SORROWS and REJOICINGS

SORROWS *and* REJOICINGS

ATHOL FUGARD

THEATRE COMMUNICATIONS GROUP
NEW YORK

Sorrows and Rejoicings is published by Theatre Communications Group, Inc. 355 Lexington Ave., New York, NY 10017-6603

The author would like to acknowledge Professor Marianne McDonald of the University of California, San Diego, for her fine Ovid translations.

Karoo photograph is reprinted by permission of Satour.

This publication is made possible in part with public funds from the New York State Council on the Arts, a State Agency.

TCG books are exclusively distributed to the book trade by Consortium Book Sales and Distribution, 1045 Westgate Dr., St. Paul, MN 55114.

LIBRARY OF CONGRESS CATALOGING-IN-PUBLICATION DATA

Fugard, Athol.
Sorrows and rejoicings / by Athol Fugard. — 1st ed.
p. cm.
ISBN 1-55936-208-1 (pbk. : alk. paper)
1. Triangles (Interpersonal relations)—Drama. 2. Women—South Africa—Drama. 3. Karoo (South Africa)—Drama. 4. Women, Black—Drama. 5. White women—Drama. 6. Exiles—Drama. 7. Poets—Drama. I. Title.

PR 9369.3.F8 S67 2001
822'.914—dc21   2001045683
CIP

Cover photo by T. Charles Erickson
Cover and text design by Lisa Govan
First Edition, February 2002

For my sisters
Mary, Katrina and Dudu

PRODUCTION HISTORY

Sorrows and Rejoicings received its world premiere in May 2001, at the McCarter Theatre Center, Princeton, NJ (Emily Mann, Artistic Director; Jeffrey Woodward, Managing Director). The production was directed by the playwright. Associate direction, set design and costume design was by Susan Hilferty and lighting design was by Dennis Parichy. The cast was as follows:

ALLISON OLIVIER	Blair Brown
MARTA BARENDS	L. Scott Caldwell
DAWID	John Glover
REBECCA	Marcy Harriell

In August 2001, *Sorrows and Rejoicings* was produced at the Baxter Theatre Centre (Mannie Manim, Director) at the University of Cape Town in South Africa. The production was directed by the playwright. Associate direction, set design and costume design was by Susan Hilferty and lighting design was by Mannie Manim. The cast was as follows:

ALLISON OLIVIER	Jennifer Steyn
MARTA BARENDS	Denise Newman
DAWID	Marius Weyers
REBECCA	Amrain Ismail-Essop

In February 2002, *Sorrows and Rejoicings* was produced at Second Stage Theatre in New York City (Carole Rothman, Artistic Director; Carol Fishman, Managing Director). The production was directed by the playwright. Associate direction, set design and costume design was by Susan Hilferty and lighting design was by Dennis Parichy. The cast was as follows:

ALLISON OLIVIER	Judith Light
MARTA BARENDS	Charlayne Woodard
DAWID	John Glover
REBECCA	Marcy Harriell

SORROWS and REJOICINGS

I feared I'd forget my Latin language
Forget how to use my dear mother tongue.
I thought it would clot and dry in my veins
And never again its sweet song be sung.

Now I talk to myself and speak the words
Savoring each syllable so long unused.
I speak and practice my verbal art,
Those skills they say in Rome I abused.

So I eke out my life and pass my time
Trying to erase my loss and my pain.
I spend hours in speaking my mother tongue,
In which I find both my loss and my gain.

You ask me when my lament will end:
When my exile ends and my cry is heard.
Although complaints pour from a fountain full,
It's my fate that speaks, not mine those words.
Bring me back to my land and beloved wife:
You'll hear me laugh, when you return me to life.

I wish that you mourned my death not my life,
And you would be widowed only through death.
Then my spirit could soar on the winds of my land,
Your tears on my breast as I breathed my last breath.
Your fingers then would have closed my eyes
After one last look on my native skies.

—EXCERPT FROM OVID'S *Sorrows* (TRISTIA)
TRANSLATED BY MARIANNE MCDONALD

The living room of a large and comfortable house in a Karoo village. The centerpiece is a glowing, well-polished stinkwood table and chairs.

A murmur of voices outside.

A front door opens and closes and a few seconds later three women enter the room from a passageway. They are Allison Olivier, a white woman, in her forties; Marta Barends, a colored woman, also in her forties; and Rebecca, Marta's daughter, much lighter skinned than her mother, eighteen years old.

It is immediately obvious that they have come from a funeral. Both Allison and Marta are dressed in black. Marta has a small bible and hymn book in one hand and a large bunch of keys in the other. She is the only one to move with ease and familiarity around the room.

Allison is the first to appear. She walks slowly into the room and looks around. She is alone in the room for a few seconds.

Marta then enters and stands quietly to one side. She watches Allison and waits.

Rebecca follows a few seconds later but remains at the entrance to the room. She will stay there—a sullen and silent presence in the background—until her moment toward the end of the play.

ALLISON: My word! Nothing has changed. This is exactly as I remember it.

MARTA: That's right. Nothing has changed. *(With pride)* When he left this room sixteen years ago he made a promise that he would come back, and I made a promise to him that when he did he would find that nothing had changed. He kept his promise, I kept mine. Every time I dusted and swept in here I put everything back in its place. The rest of the house also. You can go look. Nothing has changed.

ALLISON: I believe you.

MARTA: That first night when he got back, he walked in here, stopped right where you are now, looked around and said it felt like he had never been gone.

ALLISON: In some ways he hadn't. He spent a lot of those sixteen years in London dreaming about being back here, in the village, in this house, this room.

MARTA: Ja, I also had dreams like that.

(Marta takes off her hat and places it, her bible, hymn book and large bunch of keys on a small side table.)

Would you like a cup of tea, Allison?

ALLISON: Thank you, but no. I won't stay long. I just wanted to see the house again . . . and have a few last words with you before leaving.

(An awkward pause.)

MARTA: There was twenty-five people there at the grave and that's not counting us and old Jaap and Frik, our two grave diggers. That makes thirty all together.

ALLISON: As many as that!

MARTA: I counted them: Old Retief and his wife and son, Mr. and Mrs. De Lange, the Conradies, Scheepers, the Vosloo sisters, Dominee Weyers and his wife and then my people from the location.

ALLISON: That tall elderly man who came up to me afterwards and shook my hand . . .

MARTA: The colored man in the brown suit?

ALLISON: Yes.

MARTA: Mr. Sarel Bosman. He was just a schoolteacher when you first met him; now he's the principal of our school and also our mayor.

ALLISON: Yes, of course! I thought I recognized him.

MARTA: Ja, Dawid and he were good friends. Whenever Dawid came to the village there was always a visit to the school, a cup of tea with Mr. Bosman and then a talk to the children, what Mr. Bosman was always calling "Dawid's pep talk."

ALLISON *(Eagerly)*: I went with David on one of those visits. I can still see him! . . . standing there in the classroom, fired-up with passionate conviction, his little audience sitting cross-legged on the floor, barefoot and bright-eyed, staring up at the strange white man who was talking to them about courage and having faith in the future. Because their world was going to change! They were going to have chances their mothers and fathers never had!

It reminded me of the very first time I saw him. The Wit's campus in 1976—on the steps of the great hall. A huge student rally in support of the Soweto Uprising. But that time he made twenty-year-old Allison Fogarty very nervous. His combination of passion and politics left me in no doubt that I was watching one of those evil agitators the Government was warning us about. *(Smiles at the memory)*

I was actually relieved when the police finally moved in and dragged him off to a police van. A few weeks later I was in the main lecture theatre when in walked that same dangerous agitator to lecture us, and with the same conviction and passion on the poetry of W. B. Yeats *(A pause while she remembers)*:

> The wind is old and still at play
> While I must hurry on my way
> For I am running to paradise.

At the end of that lecture Allison Fogarty was in love.

MARTA: Mr. Bosman has a picture of the two of them hanging on the wall in his office. They got their arms around each other. You can sommer see they was good friends. I snapped it. The last time he was down here just before you and him left the country.

ALLISON: I must visit the school tomorrow before I go back. Is it still up there on the hill?

MARTA: Same place. Same old building. Government keeps promising us money to do it up, but I'll believe it when I see it.

ALLISON: I think I also recognized some of the white faces there at the graveside. They certainly did stare at us didn't they.

MARTA: But of course. They was waiting to see if we was going to cry and who would cry first, the wife or that colored woman of his.

ALLISON: We disappointed them.

MARTA *(Bitter pride)*: I hope so. I wasn't going to give that lot any satisfaction. They've been staring at me like that since the day Rebecca was born. They all know who her father was.

ALLISON: Were you expecting that many people to turn up?

MARTA: But of course. Why not?

ALLISON: Well, he'd only been back in the village for . . . what? . . .

MARTA: Twenty-nine days.

ALLISON: . . . After being away for sixteen years. I just thought people might have forgotten him by now.

MARTA: Not in the Karoo. Vriend of vyand—Friends or enemies—the people you love or the people you hate, we don't forget them. All of those people there in the graveyard, white and colored, knew him and his family. Olivier was a big name here in the valley once upon a time. Even today, mention it at one of the ladies' tea parties and in no time they are all shaking their heads and talking about the big kudu bull that jumped on the car killing his mother and father and the little two-year-old boy that came back here to grow up with his ouma and oupa.

Haai Siestog! Those two old people worshiped him. And so did my mother! Ja. She was then already working in this house when it happened. Because his ouma's hands was so bad with the arthritis my mother was the one who changed our little Dawid's nappies. Ja. The colored Barends have worked in this house almost as long as the white Oliviers have lived in it. My mother was as young as that one *(Indicating Rebecca)* when she started working for them, and I first came into this room as a baby on her back. *(Turning to Rebecca)* . . . And you first came into this room on my back, my girl.

ALLISON: The big wreath of white lilies . . . who was that from?

MARTA: His Auntie Lettie. His mother's sister. Mrs. Laetitia De Wet. She's in an old-age home in Graaff-Reinet now, but they used to have a farm on the Richmond Road and a house here in the village. But you met her.

ALLISON: I did?

MARTA (*A crooked little smile*): Oh yes. Right here in this very room. You don't remember?

ALLISON: No.

MARTA: Your first visit to the village. I served you all tea in here—you, Dawid, his oupa, Mrs. De Wet and her daughter Cornelia. They had come around to meet Dawid's "bride-to-be." She didn't like you. I could read her face like a book: "Why was Dawid marrying this English girl from the city who couldn't speak Afrikaans properly? There were mos so many nice Karoo meisies who would have given anything to be Mrs. Dawid Olivier." It was very funny watching you all, you trying so hard to be nice, Dawid correcting your bad Afrikaans so that Mrs. De Wet could understand what you were saying. It didn't help. At the end of the tea party she still didn't like you. (*Pause*) Neither did I.

(*The two women look at each other frankly and un-flinchingly.*)

ALLISON: Yes, I know. I never did feel very welcome in this village.

You've got a good memory, Marta.

MARTA: There's some things you can't forget, even if you want to. That tea party was one of them for me. He had phoned beforehand of course to say he was coming down and that he was bringing someone with him ... "Someone special," he said. But I didn't think too much about it. Once or twice before he had brought a girlfriend down with him but I could see there was nothing serious between them. So at first I thought you was just another one of those. But then the tea party and suddenly there it was ... "My bride-to-be, Auntie Lettie!" My heart nearly stopped. But that's the way it is for a servant . . . scraps and leftovers from the table.

(Pause.)

"Mrs. Allison Olivier . . ." *(Uses the Afrikaans pronunciation of "Olivier")* Sorry, Allison, but no, it still doesn't sound right.

(Marta sees a little spot on the table, takes out a small handkerchief and tries to rub it away. Not satisfied with the result, she fetches a yellow dusting cloth from a cupboard and gives the table a good rub. From time to time in the course of the play she will return compulsively to polishing the table.)

ALLISON: No, it doesn't, does it. It was better in London. There they pronounced it "Allison Olivier." *(The English pronunciation)* First time I heard it I rather liked it. Gave me a sense of the new beginning we had believed London was going to be. David of course hated it. He became very paranoid about little things like that, saw them as an erosion of his Afrikaner identity.

MARTA *(Seeing her daughter standing in the doorway)*: Ag, Rebecca, stop your nonsense now and come into the room. He's gone, my girl. Dead and buried. Why don't you now also bury your anger.

(Rebecca doesn't move.)

(To Allison) A few years ago we had a big fight in here—she and me—only ten years old at the time but believe me she already knew how to use her tongue. *(To Rebecca)* You must thank him for that

you know. Ja. That's where you got it from. He was the one with the words, Rebecca, not your mother.

(Back to Allison) That time was also after a funeral, his oupa's. You should have seen the crowd at the grave for that one! *(Pause)* Right up to the very last hymn I was waiting for him, hoping he would suddenly come walking up the road to say his last good-bye to his oupa. I knew the Government had said: "No," that they wasn't going to let him come back into the country, but I was still hoping for a miracle. When it was all over she and me we came back here to tidy up. I had served tea and cake to all the old man's relatives and friends before the service. So I was polishing away and we were having this good fight. I was cross with her because she didn't join in and sing any of the hymns at the graveside—she already hated him then you see—and the next thing I know is she is calling me: "N Ou Stinkhout Meid"—"An Old Stinkwood Servant."

That's good isn't it! "Old Stinkwood Marta." I hit her—first time ever—I hit her hard and she ran out of the house crying and shouting that she would find a way to hurt me back, which she did. She also said she would never come back into this room. She hasn't. Eight years, and that *(Pointing)* is as far as she goes.

(To Rebecca as she lovingly wipes down the table) But you know something, my child, now I like the name you called me that day. Truly. You can call me that again if you like and I won't hit you. Because you were right, I am a Stinkwood Servant. Look at it, Rebecca, *(Indicates the table)* isn't it beautiful! Ja, that's stinkwood for you. If you pol-

ish and look after it and love it, it gets more and more beautiful as it gets old. Dawid loved this table. He always said he was going to write a poem about it one day. He explained it all so wonderfully to me one day when I was still a little girl:

Once upon a time it was the King of the Knysna Forest, the tallest of all the tall trees. Monkeys and beautiful birds lived in it and made their nests in it. Elephants slept underneath it at night. Then one day men came with their axes and chopped and chopped and chopped until the king came crashing down. But that wasn't the end of it because then the carpenter came and gave it a new life by making it into this beautiful table. Now it is the place where the family sits down to say grace and eat the food that God gave them. This is where the family prays. But it hasn't forgotten its life in the green forest. Yes, it's got a memory, Rebecca. Late at night when the rest of the house is asleep it remembers those days when its head was full of the songs of birds and the chattering of monkeys, when big elephant bulls rubbed up against it. And it also remembers him, how when he was here on holidays this is where he used to sit and write his poems and other things. Late at night. Candlelight . . . no electricity in those days.

Ja! He was right. This table is alive—I can feel it when I touch it. It has taught me how to wait, because it and me, we knew he would keep his promise and come back.

(The moment segues into a memory of Dawid. At first it is just his voice that we hear.)

DAWID: Marta! Marta Barends!

I'm looking for Marta Barends.
Marta? Are you there?
It's me! Dawid! Dawid Olivier!

(Dawid appears. Fifty-one years old, gaunt and drawn features, nondescript travel-weary clothes. From time to time he has to pause and close his eyes as a wave of exhaustion overcomes him. He smiles weakly.)

That's right. You're not seeing a ghost. It's me. I'm alive, and I'm here.

I know. I also can't believe it. But it's true. Dawid Olivier is finally back home. That's how I kept myself going for the past—I don't know— what?—forty-eight hours? Just kept saying to myself: "You're going home, man. Hang on! Keep moving, because you're going home." Blind, running blind, like an animal with the hounds of hell after it. Get to that place where you can stop, finally just stop and be safe.

(An exhausted little laugh, a mixture of tears and relief.)

Sorry . . . I'm rambling.

Hardest part was that damned aeroplane, eleven hours of it, half asleep, half awake. And the noise! In your ears all the time. Then the car and trying to get out of Joburg. Should have seen me! I haven't been behind a steering wheel for God alone knows how long. Nearly crashed the damned thing a couple of times. Kept having to pull over to the side of the road, rest for a few minutes then carry on again. Thank God for the place names—you know, those signboards on the side of the road—they also kept me going: Wonderboom, Rietfontein, Heuningspruit—kept saying them, over and over like a mantra, adding the new ones as they came up—Voorspoed, Kromdraai, Verkeerdevlei, Wolwehoek . . .

I was hanging on to that steering wheel like a drowning man. I knew that once I had Bloemfontein behind me I'd be all right. That is what I always used to wait for in the old days, when I drove down from Joburg for the holidays. Remember? Because after Bloemfontein the Karoo takes over you see, and sure enough there it was again as if the last sixteen years had never happened. That empty road stretching away ahead of me to the horizon, the swarms of swallows under the flyovers, the first Karoo koppies starting to rise out of the Free State vlaktes . . .

Somewhere between Colesberg and Nooupoort I pulled over, got out of the car. One of those little picnic spots . . . cement table and a couple of pepper trees, windmill and a water tank on the other side of the fence. Late afternoon, the sun still warm, a little breeze ruffling the grass . . . I just stood there and waited and then slowly it came, that sense again of being either at the beginning of time, or the end of it, the first man or the last one.

Music was never as sweet as that silence. Harmony, Marta! That's what it was. Harmony between whatever passes for a soul inside me and the world I was standing in—the lonely veld, the defiant koppies, that implacable Karoo sky . . . space, time, and silence . . . my epiphany. Could have all ended there as far as I was concerned, and who knows, maybe it did. Because I had made it, I was home. There were days in London, bad days Marta and many of them, when I thought that I would never see it again. But there I was, somewhere on the road between Colesberg and Nooupoort.

Sixteen years ago my hand would have started itching for a pencil and paper and another hopeless attempt to weave a net of words that would capture that moment. This time, I just let it be. There was a part of me that would have been quite happy if it had all ended there, but I knew it couldn't because there was still you . . . and Rebecca. My journey wasn't over. So I got back into the car and now here I am . . . and there you are! Marta Barends! Dear God, let me look at you.

No! No please. Anything you like, rather slam the door in my face, just don't cry.

(Pause.)

Allison?

No. She's still over there, somewhere in France now I think—I don't know—or Germany. All over the place. She had to go off to a conference, but yes, she's . . . she's well.

(Suddenly aware of what he looks like . . . his body, his clothing) Ja, I know, can't say that for myself. This is not quite the Dawid you remember hey.

Time, Marta, time. It's a hungry rat and it's been gnawing away at me. I know. I haven't been eating too well. You see according to the doctors I'm sick. It's got a long fancy name, but they've given me lots of medicine so I'll be all right. What I really need though is Karoo sunshine and fresh air and your cooking. That way we'll see in the millennium together.

But to hell with me, man, let me look at you properly! *(Quoting)* "Marta Barends! Warm brown bread and thorn-tree honey! Warm bruin brood en doring boom heuning." You remember? I'll write that poem this time.

Hey hey hey! Come on now. No tears remember. I kept my promise! I'm back. We must celebrate!

(Segue back to the present.)

MARTA: It was late at night. He had driven all around the location trying to find me. I still don't know how he managed to get this far. I didn't recognize him at first. He looked like a ghost standing there in the darkness. What does this old white man want, I thought to myself. But then: "Marta Barends," the way only he could say it. Anyway . . . I got dressed quickly and we came back down here. I opened the house—I've had his room ready and waiting for him all these years—and that is where he stayed until the end.

ALLISON: What do you mean?

MARTA: He never went out.

ALLISON: He never left the house?

MARTA: No.

ALLISON: Not at all?

MARTA: No. Not even to see his oupa's grave. I tried to tell him it was his . . . his plig . . . his . . .

ALLISON: His duty?

MARTA: Ja—that's the word—his duty, but he just shook his head. He already knew he was going to be lying there with his oupa in a few weeks time. Didn't want to see nobody. Not even Mr. Bosman. But he spent a lot of time at the windows looking out . . . the street, the orchard at the back, and the mountains. One time I found him at the window in the little side bedroom. You know the one? You can see the trading store from there. He made me stand there with him and tell him all about the people who was going in and coming out of the shop. Even the little children carrying their empty bottles for paraffin. He wanted to know their names and who their mommies and daddies was. Ate nothing. Just about said nothing.

I tried to make him tell me about London but he said there was nothing to tell. I felt so useless, sitting there in the bedroom with him. I could see he was sick and in pain but all he wanted me to do was tell him about the village and all the things what had happened since he was gone. And not just the important things like who got married and who had a baby and who was dead and so on, but any old rubbish that came into my head.

Like one day he asked me to tell him all the things that were on the shelves in the trading store—you know, the tins of pilchards, the packets of mealie-meal and sugar, the bottles of methylated spirit, Five Roses Tea, Koo Apricot Jam—and how much they cost. And he just lay there listening to me very hard as if I was telling him something important. And always in Afrikaans. I had to speak to him all the time in Afrikaans. *(Helpless gesture)* I didn't know what else to do for him, what he really wanted. I knew by then he was dying, but all I could do was sit and watch.

ALLISON: He was trying to make you do the impossible, Marta.

MARTA: What do you mean?

ALLISON: Cancel out his exile—those years in London. All that gossip and talk from you was a way of trying to live them over again, but this time here in the village.

MARTA: He started to get deurmekaar towards the end, you know, all mixed-up about where he was and so on. Sometimes I was even wondering if he knew who I was, but just when I was thinking like that he would say: "Marta, what is today?" And then I would tell him . . . you know . . . Monday or Tuesday or whatever it was, December so and so. Because he was counting the days, you see. He wanted so badly to live to the millennium. Did you know that?

ALLISON: No.

MARTA: Ja. Two things kept him hanging on in here . . . waiting for the millennium and waiting for her. *(Gestures to Rebecca)* I begged her to see him and to make her peace with him before he died, but she wouldn't. I couldn't tell him that, so whenever he asked about her I lied to him, said she was down in Cape Town visiting her Uncle Charlie. Not nice hey. The man you love is dying and you lie to him because his daughter hates him and doesn't want to see him.

(Rebecca listens unflinchingly.)

That's the end of the story. Dawid Olivier didn't get his last wishes.

ALLISON: It's not as bleak as that. He could have died in London.

MARTA: Ja, that's true. We must thank God he got back here. He loved this village.

ALLISON: And I could never understand why. One dusty street and a hundred houses . . . half of them empty . . . and in the middle of nowhere! Miles and miles of nothing except flat veld and little gray bushes. I was a city girl, Marta . . . and what's more, an English-speaking city girl who had to write her matric Afrikaans exam twice because she was so bad at it, and even then only managed to scrape through. As far as I was concerned I didn't belong here, didn't want to belong here, and marrying "Dawid Olivier" *(Gives the name an exaggerated Afrikaans pronunciation)* wasn't going to change any of that.

Those few times he brought me down here after we'd got married I couldn't wait for the "wonderful Karoo holiday" to end so that we could get back to Johannesburg and civilization. I used to believe it was just a case of boredom on my side— nothing to do and a whole, long, hot, fly-swatting day in which to do it. But in London I finally faced up to the truth. I was frightened of it. The Karoo, his Afrikaner world and, of course, you, it all frightened me. Deep down inside me I already knew that I was going to have to fight to keep his love . . . and I wasn't sure I would win. *(A bitter smile, she shakes her head at the memory of herself)*

Standing there in the cemetery this morning I couldn't help wondering how different it all might have been if I had understood and accepted a few things right from the beginning . . . if instead of feeling threatened by this world I had tried to understand and see it the way he did. Then it came to me to try to do just that, a sort of farewell gesture to David in place of the flowers I hadn't time to organize. See it for him, I said to myself. See it for him for the last time. So I tried. I opened myself to everything I use to hate about this place . . . to that cruel sun beating down on our heads, to the veld and koppies, to those solemn Afrikaner faces standing around the coffin with the domi-

nee's voice droning on in Afrikaans that I didn't
understand, to that donkey braying in the distance
. . . and to you standing there with a burden of
grief and love you were trying so hard to hide . . .
everything I could see or hear . . . I took it all in.
And you know something terribly sad, Marta . . . I
knew that if he had been alive and I was given
another chance now . . . I would end up loving it!

MARTA: And that would include me, Allison Olivier?

ALLISON: Oh yes, you as well, Marta Barends. And
Rebecca.

(Pause. Allison's tone changes.)

Back in London I have to take a bus every morning to the university where I teach. On the way it
passes one of those ghastly new cemeteries. You
know what I'm talking about? Rows and rows of
gravestones. Hundreds of them! He was with me
in the bus one morning, a gray wet London morning, both us with moods to match the weather . . .
I think we'd been there about five years already so
all the excitement of being "free" and in one of
the world's greatest cities had worn off. Anyway, after
we had passed the cemetery—he had been staring at
it all the time, the traffic was heavy so we were just
crawling along—he turned to me: "If anything happens to me, Allison, for my soul's sake don't bury
me in England. Get my body back home."

At first I thought it was just a joke but he
insisted that I make him that promise which of
course ended up with us having a bad argument
in that bus. A stupid argument because it had
nothing to do with what we were really feeling.
He was lonely and desperately homesick and I was

jealous . . . and beginning to feel defeated. It was
in that bus that I began to realize that no matter
what I did, no matter how hard I tried—and
believe me I tried hard—he would never think of
the place where we lived as his "home."

MARTA: He should never have left the country.

ALLISON: Yes, that was a mistake, a big mistake. But it's
easy to say that now. At the time it seemed as if we
had no choice.

MARTA: It was all that politics that got him into trouble.

ALLISON: That is perfectly true, and David would have
been the first to agree with you.

MARTA: So? He should have left it alone.

ALLISON: His conscience wouldn't let him.

MARTA: Dawid Olivier was meant to be a poet, not a
politician.

ALLISON: And he would have told you that in this country you can't separate the two. Without people like
him, Marta, you would still be living in the old
South Africa.

MARTA: Wrong, Allison. I still am. Go walk around the
village tomorrow and see how much of the "new
South Africa" you can find. Dawid, who knew this
village, would be the first person to say I am right.

(Pause. Allison doesn't want to argue.)

So then it *was* your idea.

ALLISON: What was my idea?

MARTA: To leave the country. You persuaded him to go.

ALLISON: No I didn't. *(A sudden flare of anger and impa-
tience)* But for God's sake! . . . suppose I had.
Wasn't it my right and responsibility to do that if I
believed it was the best thing for him. I was his
wife, Marta! . . . and I also loved him. *(Pause)* But if

you really want to know, it wasn't "my idea" and I certainly didn't persuade him to do it. I wouldn't have succeeded. You of all people should know that David had a mind of his own. We talked about it of course, but it was finally his decision. I would have done whatever he wanted . . . stayed here or followed him . . . anywhere! Those last years in Johannesburg weren't easy you know, and we knew they were going to get worse. That banning order was only the beginning.

MARTA *(Defiantly)*: Well *I* tried to persuade him *not* to go—his last visit when they let him come down here to say good-bye to his oupa. He tried very hard to make me believe he was doing the right thing . . . but no! . . . I didn't . . . but I also didn't know how to argue with him about those things. I just kept on having this feeling that it was wrong, that it was not the right thing to do, but . . .

(Marta makes a helpless gesture. The moment segues into another memory of Dawid . . . this time it is the thirty-six-year-old man full of energy and passionate conviction who is at the point of leaving the country. He talks to Marta.)

DAWID: Yes, it is my decision. I am doing it because I know it is the right thing to do. And I am also not the first one to believe that. Half of the comrades are already over there. No! Don't shake your head like that. Listen to this: *(Reads from a little slender paperback book:)*

My message will travel to all the people
All over the world my charge will be heard

From where the sun rises to the where the
    sun sets
Both East and West will witness my word.
Over the earth and across vast seas
Shall the sound of my outcry be great.
Not only the present will know your crime,
Indicted forever will be your fate.

Those lines were written just a few years after
Christ was born by Publius Ovidius Naso—Ovid for
short. Roman poet who was also forced into exile.

All over the world my charge will be heard.

That is what I am going to try to do, Marta. That is
why I am leaving the country. My writing is the
only weapon I've got. Without it I'm useless. And
that is what that bloody banning order has made
me . . . useless! I can't be read. I can't be published. I can't be quoted. You know what comes
next? "So why bother to write, Dawid Olivier?"
    Ja. I'd reached a point where I was actually
asking myself that question. "Why bother? You
know they'll just wake you up again in the middle
of the night, search the place, find the manuscript
and take it away like all the other stuff they've
looted from your life." Exile is going to give me
back my voice, Marta. In London I'll have the freedom again to speak and be heard, to write and be
read.
    I am not running away. I'm leaving because
I want to fight, Marta . . . for you, for our Rebecca,
for those children I spoke to in that miserable little classroom this morning. Do you think I could
live with the memory of those eager little faces

staring up at me, listening to what I was saying, if I wasn't certain that I was doing the right thing? God, Marta, there was so much hunger in that little room! And not just for food, which none of them ever get enough of, hunger for something just as important as bread and apricot jam—Hope! When our little Rebecca's turn comes to sit in that classroom I want hers to be a life full of hope. Her world has got to be better than the one we grew up in.

I went through a bad time just before I made up my mind last week to take that exit permit they've been dangling in front of my nose like a carrot. I was very depressed . . . morbid . . . all sorts of dark fantasies. One morning when I was alone in the flat—Allison was at work—I had an idea for a little short story. A man, one of the comrades, is in a similar situation—banned and silenced into impotence by the Government. There is nothing left for him to do except sit in his comfortable little flat and listen to classical music, read beautiful poetry and watch the world around him go up in flames on his television set . . . Me! His sense of uselessness is finally too much for him. He cuts off his testicles, puts them in a box and posts them to the prime minister with a little note: "You took away my manhood, so why not take these as well." That's when I knew I had to leave.

(Pause.)

Yes, Allison agrees. She's been very strong. It hasn't been easy for her either you know. Those bastards have done their best to intimidate her and break up our marriage. She's been taken in for questioning several times. They've even tried to get her fired from her job in the library. Thanks to my banning order she's also hardly got a life left. If someone comes around to see her I've got to scramble for the bedroom. Ja. Three people is legally a gathering, and my banning order doesn't allow me to attend gatherings. They only let me come down here because they know now that I'm going and because I said I wanted to say good-bye to my grandfather. And you as well! For God's sake, Marta, you know that. But I couldn't tell them that.

No, please! Don't make it hard for me. I need your faith, Marta. I need you to believe that I'll come back. Because I will. I swear it. Those bastards won't last much longer. I'll be back. Wait for me.

(Segue back into the present.)

ALLISON: We went over there with such high hopes. God, it was exciting! London! And freedom! Freedom for him to say and write whatever he liked. Freedom from fear. For the first time I realized just how much fear we had lived with in South Africa . . . fear of the informer, fear of that knock on your door in the middle of the night, fear of him being taken in for one hundred and eighty days of interrogation and solitary confinement . . . several of our comrades had been broken that way. But the most wonderful thing of all about London was just watching him come back to life and start living again. That last year in Johannesburg was hell. He had become very depressed and had completely stopped writing, just sat around in that little Hillbrow flat all day brooding and bitter. That's where he learnt how to stand at a window for hours on end looking out at the world.

London changed all of that. I was once again with the man I loved and had married. Our very first shopping expedition was in search of a stationery store for writing material—paper, notebooks and pencils. After that we worried about groceries. He was like a child in a toy shop . . . feeling the paper, comparing sizes of notebooks, because there had to be one for his pocket and one for his desk, and then of course the ink for his pen . . . blue? Or black? What about violet? . . . But in the end it was back to his favorite . . . brown, with just a touch of red in it: "The color of dry blood, my dear Allison, because that is what a writer leaves on the page." I've still got those first notebooks. And he got a job without any trouble—teaching English at a posh school. It all seemed perfect.

At night, after supper, we would clear away the dishes and he would settle down to his writing. He was very fond of a Latin poet called Ovid, who had also gone into exile and had written a book of poems about it. David's idea was to match that book with one of his own . . . he was going to dedicate it to you, Rebecca. The Latin book is called *Sorrows*, because for Ovid that is all that exile meant; David was going to call his book *Rejoicings*. It was going to be a book in celebration of freedom, the freedom he had found in London and which he believed would one day finally arrive in South Africa. He even had a publisher waiting for it! He already had a small reputation in London thanks to the poems that had been published in magazines and in that anthology of South African poetry.

And it was just as good for me—maybe even better. Those first few months in that shabby bed-sitter in Finchley Road were the happiest of all the time we lived together. In that pokey little room with its shilling-a-time gas heater I finally had David all to myself.

Did you ever know how jealous I was of you, Marta?

MARTA: Jealous? Of me?

ALLISON: Yes. From the very first time I saw you, trying to be a servant and David trying to be the master, I knew there was something between the two of you. And then when I saw little Rebecca on your back I knew for sure. Poor David! He made it so obvious by deliberately ignoring the child when she was in here with you.

MARTA: I could see you didn't like me. But jealous? Ag, no Allison. You were wasting your time being jealous of me—you with all your education and a white skin. I had nothing to give him . . . except trouble and a daughter who doesn't love him.

ALLISON: No, Marta. You had as much to give him as I ever did . . . and maybe even more. It has taken me a long time to be able to say that, but it's true. Apart from being the woman you are, you are also a part of this world that he loved with such passion. You are this world, Marta, in a way that I could never be, no matter how hard I tried . . . and the truth is I didn't try at all. At the time I refused to see that. I refused to see what bound the two of you together. As far I was concerned you were right: you did have nothing to give him except an illegitimate child and big trouble if the two of you were ever caught as lovers.

MARTA: So what did he say?

ALLISON: When?

MARTA: When you told him that?

ALLISON: I never did. Just thought it to myself.

MARTA: You never talked about me?

ALLISON: Only as "dear Marta the faithful, loyal and devoted servant and friend of the family." At the time I fooled myself that I was being sensitive to his feelings, but the truth is I was afraid of what I would find if I started probing and tried to challenge your place in his life.

(Pause.)

There's something I've always wanted to ask you. Did he make love to you during those visits when I was here with him?

MARTA: Didn't you ever ask him?

ALLISON: Yes, I did.

MARTA: What did he say?

ALLISON: No. He said no.

MARTA: So why do you ask me?

ALLISON: Because I've never been sure if I could believe him.

MARTA *(After a pause)*: Not when you were here with him. Do you want to know about the other times?

ALLISON: No.

It wasn't easy for me you know. The situation was so damned complicated. Because let's face it, if everything had been different, if this had been a free country back then, mightn't he have married you? Had I got him, like so many other things in my life, because in addition to all my other splendid virtues, I had a white skin? It's called "liberal guilt," Marta, and I suffered from an overdose of it.

MARTA *(Shaking her head)*: Haai, Allison! . . . and there was I jealous also, hating you because you had taken him away from me.

ALLISON: *(With a wry little laugh at herself)*: Yes, I also thought I had done that, and to make quite certain of it, I decided in London that we would have a family of our own. We had talked about having children in Johannesburg because we both wanted them, but we both also felt that the situation in the country was too dangerous for us to do anything about it. London was different. We were starting a new life! He had a well-paid teaching post, wonderful prospects for his writing, and best of all you were ten thousand miles away. Thanks to that one-way exit permit and the way things were going in the country it looked as if it was going to be a long time before he would see you and Rebecca again.

(Pause. Marta waits expectantly.)

He got mumps.

MARTA: Pampoentjies?

ALLISON: Yes, that's what he called it. Little pumpkins?

MARTA: Ja. Because of the swellings.

ALLISON: Yes, he certainly had those. At the time we didn't know what the consequences could be—in fact we had a few good laughs at it—his testicles came up as big as cricket balls. Anyway, to cut a long story short that was the end of our hopes for a family. I made the mistake once of suggesting that we should think about adopting a child. He said no, he already had a child of his own . . . waiting for him back "home." So I went back to school—London University for a Ph.D.—and David started drinking.

Oh, Marta! . . . what a bloody mess it ended up being. And why? Mumps? Can "little pumpkins" destroy a relationship? A life? Was it me? Or you maybe? Or once again just a case of good old South Africa doing what it does best . . . wrecking everything, because that is what we finally had to face up to—our life together had become a shambles.

(Pause. The moment segues into Allison's memory of Dawid after a few years in London. He has obviously had too much to drink but is still in control of all his faculties. His appearance is unkempt, suggesting an advanced degree of personal neglect.)

DAWID: A fly for God's sake. Musca domestica . . . the common housefly! Yes . . . you know—zzzzzzzz . . . *(Slaps an imaginary fly on his face)* Is that asking for too much? One miserable little fly. I had everything ready. *(Produces an empty matchbox, opens and closes it)* My ingenious little trap. I had it all worked out: sneak up on it slowly while it was washing its face with its little legs . . . staying downwind all the time . . . freezing when it looked as if it sensed danger . . . then when I was near enough—POUNCE!—and snap shut.

It was going to be a little Christmas surprise for you, my darling. Got the idea this morning after you had so tellingly slammed the front door on me and my hangover and gone off to work. I lay on in bed brooding on the melancholy state of our affairs . . . you know—marriage, finances, etc., etc. . . . and the general fuck-up of the world as it limps along to the end of the century. All was quiet in here except, very appropriately, for the gutters which were gurgling and dribbling yet again with London misery. I didn't need a window to know that another gray, damp day was waiting for me outside. So—surprise! surprise!—I thought of what that moment would be like back home. The blinding, brazen sunlight when you opened the front door and stepped out into the street, that fatal blue sky overhead and, of course, immediately . . . yes, you guessed it. Flies! *(Waving away swarms of imaginary flies)* Flies! Flies! Flies for Africa.

I sat bolt upright in bed. Eureka! I've found it! "Gird your loins, Dawid Olivier, and go hunting. Prove to your deeply doubting mate that you are still a man. Bring home your trophy, release it in your cheerless little world to buzz around busily while we guzzle Algerian plonk and sing 'Auld Lang Syne.'" But alas . . . home is the hunter, home from the streets of London town, but his matchbox is empty. Couldn't find any.

One little fly! That is all I wanted. Millions of them back home. Billions. Beating their brains out against windowpanes all day long—their little corpses laid out at the bottom on the sill at the end of the day. You try writing a poem in the Karoo without a fly swatter on the table. Impossible. Whack! Whack! Whack! And then at night the moths: the windows are open to let in the cool of the evening, so in they come, as soft as whispered secrets . . . little moths, big moths . . . crashing into the Coleman lamp, immolating themselves in the candle flame. I used to feel guilty! So many little sacrifices for one little poem . . . it better be good! Ja.

Outside that open window the big black African night, dogs barking in the location, crickets blinking outside in the dark like little fallen stars. *(Pause)* No! No head shaking. Don't think I am wasting my time, Mrs. Allison Olivier *(The English pronunciation)*. There's a nice little poem hidden away in all this, you know. The only problem is, how the hell does a cry of despair, because that is what it would be if I wrote it, how does that fit into a volume called *Rejoicings?* Come to think of it though, is there anything left in my life that could be an occasion for rejoicing? And even if by some miracle there was, doesn't look as if I'd be able to do anything about it, does it. Do you know how long it has been since I've written a line about anything? The ink in my fountain pen has clotted and dried up like the blood in a dead man's veins. God knows I've tried to get it flowing again but if my writing ever had a heart it has stopped beating. I'm drought-stricken . . . an officially declared drought-stricken area.

I watched it happen to the Karoo a couple of times, you know. A long, lingering agony as a relentless sun burnt everything to death. Day after day. A little taste of the inner circle of Dante's *Inferno.* Even thorntrees and the aloes were dead at the end of it. There was eventually renewal of course. The rains did finally come. There's a poem by Hopkins in which he cries out: "Lord of my soul, send my roots rain!" . . . Or something like that. Is that what I should do? Pray and wait for Divine mercy? *(Pause)*

And stop drinking? *(A good laugh)* Dammit! Why did I give you that opening!

How do you do it Allison? I mean, apart from the misery of living with me, you seem to be so together. You go off to the university every morn-

ing, study hard, write exams . . . and get the top
marks! . . . come home in the evening and sit down
and uncomplainingly eat the garbage I've cooked
up for supper in an attempt to justify my existence.
You're not fooling me are you? I mean . . . it's not
just all appearance is it? *(He studies her)* No, you're
not. Allison Olivier *(English pronunciation)* is going
to survive exile. In fact, she is going to flourish.

(Abandoning his games) That is what scares the
hell out of me you know. *(Out of the pocket of his
shapeless tweed sports coat he removes the now dog-
eared book of Ovid's poetry we saw in the farewell
scene with Marta)* He never saw his home again.
He died in exile. Caesar never relented. But worst
of all . . . his poetry died before he did. *(He reads:)*

> My talent, which at its best was only slight,
> Has rusted now and lost its sheen.
> A fertile field without the plough,
> Grows only grass and thorns and spleen.
> I fear I'm not the man I was,
> And I was little even then.
> Long suffering dulls the sharpest wit:
> There's no edge left to tongue or pen.

(Pause, then quietly) We made a mistake, Allison.
Marta was right. We should never have left.
I would have survived solitary confinement back
home. I won't survive freedom here.

(Segue back to the present.)

ALLISON: So you see, I have also been a witness to a
slow death—only my vigil is measured in years, not

in weeks. That is how long it took for that fire in him to die out and turn to ash. I tried everything I could to keep it alive, make it flare up again—everything I had as a woman to give, my love, my caring, my anger . . . God! The stupidity and waste of it all made me so angry and resentful! There were days when I hated him as much as I had ever loved him. But in the end, like you in this house, all I could do was watch and grieve and poison my own life with self-recriminations.

MARTA: Then why didn't he come back earlier? When they let Mandela out of jail all the other exiles started coming back. They would have given him a passport as well. Did you stop him?

ALLISON: Oh for God's sake, Marta! Do we have to go on thinking about each other in that way? He's dead. We buried him this morning.

MARTA: I'm sorry, Allison . . . it's just that *(A helpless gesture)* . . . hating you has become a habit.

ALLISON: Anyway the answer to your question is no. I didn't "stop" him from going back. If you really want to know I tried everything I could to persuade him to do that. And he didn't need a passport. He already had one! Yes. When he heard his oupa was dying, he applied for one and got it. Your prayers were nearly answered. You nearly saw him at his grandfather's funeral.

MARTA: But I got a letter from him saying that the Government had refused him permission . . .

ALLISON: A lie. He got his passport without any trouble.

MARTA: Then why? . . .

ALLISON: Isn't it obvious.

MARTA: No.

ALLISON: Shame.

MARTA: Dawid? Skaamte?

ALLISON: He was ashamed of himself, Marta. Of what had happened to his life. Wasted! The thought of standing at the graveside of that beautiful old man who had had so much faith in him was more than he could deal with. And then you. The thought of facing you was probably the most painful of all. That letter he wrote, telling you that he had been refused permission to return to the country, was a lie.

MARTA: It was the last letter I got from him. I also thought you had stopped him writing to me.

ALLISON: No, I didn't. By then I had stopped trying to do anything for him. Like you, I also finally realized I was helpless.

After his oupa's death his occasional bouts of heavy drinking turned into one long pub-crawling binge in the company of a bunch of other lost exiled souls. It was disgusting. They were like a pack of hyenas scavenging the headlines for bad news and waiting for South Africa to drown in the blood bath everybody was predicting. He did try a couple of times to pull himself together. There was one really serious attempt when he lost his job at the fancy school for being drunk in the classroom. But in some ways that was even worse, because then I had to watch him sit and wait . . . "for a little spark, my dear, that will ignite my imagination once again." It never came.

I stayed with him as long as I could but eventually it was too much for me. The break finally came in '94 . . . April . . . the day we had to cast our absentee ballots in South Africa's first ever democratic elections. We had agreed to meet outside the embassy in London where the voting was to take place. After that we were going to go out and have lunch together. He never showed up. I waited for a couple of hours, then cast my vote and went back to work. He turned up later that night . . . dead drunk. I didn't even ask if he had voted, and he never told me. The next day I packed my suitcases and moved out into a place of my own.

MARTA: Ja, you are right. Skaamte. That's why he wouldn't go out of the house. He was hiding away.

ALLISON: And then finally the leukemia. If it wasn't for that you might never have seen him again. Oh yes. He could so easily have wasted away the rest of his life in London. But that leukemia did what my love couldn't do, what the memories and dreams about you and the Karoo couldn't do—it sobered him up.

Even though I had moved out I still stayed in touch with him . . . we usually talked on the phone at least once a week or so or had a meal together. I couldn't bring myself around to start talking about a divorce. Maybe I was also hoping for a miracle! Anyway, he'd never mentioned the fainting fits he'd been having, so when I called as usual one day and got no reply and called again and again and still no reply, I got a little anxious. I went around to see him and there he was, stone-cold sober . . . and very frightened. What he didn't tell me was that the doctors had given him just a couple of months. I took him along for his first few treatments and then I had to go to the continent for a conference and study tour. When I got back, he was gone. There was a letter waiting for me . . . two little sentences: "I'm going home, Allison. Please forgive me." You know the rest.

MARTA: All these years I never allowed myself to think about how it would all end. But if I had, I wouldn't have imagined this. Haai! . . . life is full of surprises, hey Allison. So there . . . all over.

(Marta folds the yellow duster and steps back to admire the table.)

That is how I want to remember it—shining with love. Ja . . . and this room. Nothing changed in here since the day he left. This is where I got to know him, this was our whole world . . . the one outside was closed to us . . . skinny little colored girl from the location and the handsome young white man. I worshiped him. He used to help me with my homework. Made me bring my schoolbooks and sit at this table and do my sums and write my composition. When I was old enough to understand he would also read me his poems. And talk! Walk around this room and talk about all sorts of things, 'specially how the world was going to change one day and things would be better for everybody. Yes, you are right. There was a fire inside him and little Marta Barends warmed her life by sitting as close to it as she could. I suppose some people would say she got too close . . . and got burnt.

ALLISON: Would you have wanted anything different, Marta?

MARTA: No! Only more. I would have only prayed for more . . . more of everything, the good and the bad.

(Marta turns to Rebecca who has been a sullen listening presence in the background the whole time:)

I was your age when I first knew I loved him. How it hurt, that love! Because what could I hope for?

Nothing! . . . and that only made me love him more. It happened when his ouma died and he came down from Johannesburg for the funeral. Dawid got permission from the university to stay on here after the funeral to comfort and help his oupa. I was already then in charge of the house. So after I had given them supper, and the old man had gone to bed, he would sit in here and write and I would pretend to be busy doing things so that I could be near him. One night he was very excited by the idea he had for a new poem . . . walking around and talking about it . . . it was another one about the Karoo, about Karoo names . . . you know, of places and people and things like that . . . so he started playing games with my name . . . Marta Barends . . . Haai! The way he said it! . . . like he was tasting and eating it . . . Marta Barends!

That night we made love for the first time. Ja. This room that you hate so much, that man that you hate so much . . . in here. You were conceived in here. You owe your life to this room. *(Speaking now with bitter grief)* So say good-bye to it, Rebecca!

ALLISON: Marta . . .

MARTA *(Ignoring Allison)*: Are you happy now? You wished for him to be dead and now he is. You hate this room and this house, and now you'll never see them again. When I lock up today, that will be the end of it for us in here. I'll give the keys to Allison.

ALLISON: Marta . . . please . . .

(Marta and Rebecca ignore Allison's attempts to intervene.)

MARTA: You lucky girl! All your wishes have come true. I'm so jealous, Rebecca . . . because mine hasn't. Every night since his return I have gone down on my knees and prayed: "Dear God, please let him live to the millennium, and please, dear God, put forgiveness in Rebecca's heart so that he can see his daughter before he dies . . . then you can take him." But no.

(Marta turns away with a helpless gesture and wipes away silent tears. Allison goes to her and puts an arm around her shoulders.)

REBECCA *(Finally breaking her silence)*: He did, Mommy!

(Pause.)

He saw his daughter.

MARTA: What are you saying?

REBECCA: He saw me. In here. The night before he died.

MARTA: Don't play games with me, Rebecca!

REBECCA: I'm not. I came here. Every day since he came back I've been wanting to come here and stand in front of him . . . but not with forgiveness in my heart. I wanted to tell him what he had done to you, Mommy. I wanted to tell him how you have wasted your life waiting for him—sweeping and dusting and cleaning in here every day as if he was coming back tomorrow. I wanted to tell him that his beautiful stinkwood table wasn't shining from the Cobra wax polish, but from the tears you rubbed into it. I'm not talking poetry. Real tears. Yours. I saw them in your eyes. I saw them run down your cheeks and splash on the table when you was polishing and talking to him.

Ja, do you know you do that? Talk to him as if he was here in the room with you? I've heard you—many times—when you thought you was alone in here. You tell me there are ghosts in here . . . well I believe you and you know why? Because I've seen one. You! That's what you've become . . . the ghost of a stinkwood servant looking after her dead masters and madams.

And I wanted to tell him that I was praying for the day when he would be gone so that the house could be sold and then some other white family's "Stinkwood Marta" could come and start polishing the table. And who knows, if she's lucky maybe one day that white "master" will notice that she's got nice legs and tits and fuck her and another little bastard with light skin and straight hair will be born for everybody to point at and whisper about . . . because that, Mr. Dawid Olivier, was your only contribution to the new South Africa, Mr. Dawid Olivier . . . 'n spook kind *(Afrikaans)*, a freak . . . and she is standing here in front of you.

(Pause.)

That's why I came here that night. I knew you were here in the house, Mommy, and I wanted to say those things in front of you so that you could hear them as well. That way you would maybe wake up and see what he has done to you.

(Pause.)

I could see the light was on in here so I knocked and waited, but nobody came to the door. A part of me was very frightened. I nearly turned around and went home. But I said to myself, No, I must do it, so I just let myself in.

I didn't think it was him at first . . . I don't know what I was expecting but not the sick old white man who could hardly walk and didn't seem to know where he was . . .

(The moment segues into Rebecca's memory of Dawid. He is the sick, dying man we saw at the beginning of the play, but now in pajamas and a dressing gown. He comes shuffling forward. He is disoriented.)

DAWID: Hello. Was that you knocking? Wasn't sure if I was dreaming it . . . or where I was . . . but yes *(Looking around the room)* . . . yes of course . . . for a moment I thought I was still back in London.

Are you looking for Marta? She's asleep . . . back there in my room, in a chair. Poor woman. I'm hanging on too long. You . . . you can go through to her if you want to . . . down the passage . . . on the left . . .

(Overcome by a wave of weakness, he gropes for a chair and sits down at the table.)

Ja . . . I was dreaming again . . . back in London . . . our very first bed-sitter in Finchley Road . . . making a terrible mess of a New Zealand lamb curry I was trying to cook for my oupa . . . he was sitting there in a chair, his hands resting in his lap, his face as weathered and beautiful as Karoo rock, waiting patiently for me to say something . . . the reason for my panic was that I wanted to ask his forgiveness for not being there at his funeral . . . I wanted to make up for it by promising him that

when I died I would be buried with him and Ouma
. . . but I couldn't remember any Afrikaans . . .
I didn't want to speak to him in English, but
I couldn't find the Afrikaans words I needed.

Don't need Freud or Jung to work that one
out, do we. Of all the fears I lived with over there,
that was the worst. Dying in exile was one thing,
but living in exile without your soul? Because that
is what it would have been, not so? I mean, your
soul speaks with your mother's tongue. Couple of
times I went out and just walked aimlessly around
London streets speaking in Afrikaans to myself.
Non-stop! People must have thought me mad. But
I was holding onto my soul you see. Ovid knew all
about that as well.

When I landed in Joburg and spoke Afrikaans
to the immigration officer it was like kissing my
grandmother again, or Marta, or little Suikerbekkie—that was my nickname for her—my daughter Rebecca. Do you know her? Marta called her
Bekkie, so I called her Suikerbekkie. *(Pathetic
attempt at a little song)* "Suikerbekkie ek will jou
he . . ."

She's down in Cape Town. Last time I saw her
she was still a little baby in my lap . . . *(Pause)*
I mean, what do I say to her? I don't even know
how she feels about me. When I ask Marta she
suddenly gets very busy and mutters a few clichés.
It's obvious she's lying to me which I suppose
means there is anger and resentment. I don't
blame her. I would be. And more. I'd disown him.
A white man's bastard in the "new South Africa"?

Sorry, I don't mean to be offensive. But it's
true isn't it? You see, on my last visit before leaving the country—I was in here playing with her—

one year old! Marta had gone out to buy something. I was feeling very guilty. I knew it wasn't
going to be easy for her, that I could so easily be a
curse on her life rather than the blessing a father
was supposed to be. So what did I do? I made her
a promise! *(A little laugh)*

If you knew me you would also laugh. But
I did mean it: "I'll make you proud of me,
Rebecca. I promise. This world is going to change
and when it does, I'll come back and you will be
proud of me because I will have worked for that
change. My writing will be part of a better world."
One year old, in my lap, didn't understand a word
I was saying of course but that didn't matter. The
words were out there. The promise had been
made. (*Pause*)

I've tried everything I can to forget that
moment in here with her. Nothing is as damning a
measure of my life and its failure as that promise
I made to my little daughter . . . and didn't keep.
All I want to do now is tell her about it. I'm not
asking for her forgiveness. I don't expect it. To tell
you the truth I don't really care one way or the
other. Because it won't help. I'll never forgive
myself. I want to tell her because that pathetic little confession is all I've got left, and it belongs to
her. Nothing for Marta and Allison. Any case, they
know me now for what I am. But Rebecca . . .
maybe she can make something of it.

(Pause.)

Do you know what day it is? . . . Tuesday . . . sev-
enth, right? . . . I'm counting . . . twenty-four days
left! Marta says there's going to be a big party, a

millennium braaivleis—Karoo chops and boerewors for everybody "regardless of race, color or
creed." *(A weak little laugh)*

Moving isn't it . . . the young "new South
Africa" standing on its still wobbly legs but deter-
mined to march fearlessly into another thousand
years of recorded history! I'm trying to make it—
add my death rattle to the sounds of jubilation
when it arrives. Least I can do. But if I don't . . .
too bad!

(Dawid starts to leave and then turns back.)

If you should see Rebecca tell her that her father . . .
(Pause) No . . . no . . . never mind.

*(Dawid goes shuffling off. The moment segues back
into the present.)*

MARTA: You didn't tell him who you were? *(Rebecca, now
seated at the table, is fighting back tears)* Did you
speak to him at all? *(Rebecca shakes her head. A few
seconds of silence)* I would have given my life for
the chance you had that night. He was trying to
make peace with himself and you could have
helped him do that. Was it so hard for you? All
you had to say was: "Father, I am Rebecca."
REBECCA: What's the matter with you, Mommy! Don't
you understand anything? You taught me never to
say that word! Have you forgotten? No "father," no
"daddy," no "pa" ". . . because we must protect
him, Rebecca." Have you forgotten the little girl
who came crying to you because the other children had been teasing her again?

"Who is your daddy, Rebecca?"

"Where is your daddy, Rebecca?"

Have you forgotten wiping away her tears—and yours!—and telling her the big secret about who she was which was no secret at all because everybody knew? Have you forgotten making her promise that when he came back one day she would pretend she didn't know who he was?

Well I kept my promise, Mommy. But it wasn't easy, because if you really want to know something, when I stood there in front of him I wanted to say it. Yes, I wanted to say "Father" more than I've wanted to say anything in my whole life. But I didn't! Because you had taught me I mustn't.

(Pause.)

You've been so blind and selfish. All you've ever thought about was your own precious love. You've sacrificed your life for it and you would do that to mine as well if I let you. No, Mommy, I am not going to. I am going to live my own life the way I want to.

(Pause. Her anger is spent. She approaches her mother hesitantly in a timid attempt at reconciliation.)

You're right, Mommy, he's dead and buried. So why don't you now try to live your own life as well. Stop dreaming in here. Say good-bye to this house and its ghosts. There's nothing left for you in here. Lock up like you say, give her your big bunch of keys and come back to the location with me. There's a real life waiting for you there, with real people, our people.

ALLISON *(Quietly)*: She's right, Marta. You have still got
a whole life ahead of you and you've got to live it.

(To Rebecca) But you can't say your good-byes
to this house as easily as that Rebecca. Your mother
is going to have to carry that bunch of keys a little
bit longer. Because the house is going to be yours.

MARTA: What do you mean, Allison?

ALLISON: Exactly what I said. Rebecca is going to inher-
it the house and everything in it. One of the things
David had wanted to do when he discovered that
he had leukemia was make a will. We had a long
talk about it at the time and agreed that he should
leave the house and everything in it to Rebecca.
As it turned out he never got around to doing that
but I know that is what he wanted . . . and I will see
that it happens. It will be left in trust to you, Marta,
until she turns twenty-one . . . which will be in three
years, right? I'll get lawyers on it as soon as I get
back to London. I was going to talk to you about
it earlier but things got a little out of hand . . . and
maybe that was just as well.

(To Rebecca) You can sell it, you and your
mother can live in it . . . you can do anything you
like with it. It's yours.

(Pause.)

In return there is something I want from you,
Marta. His early poems. He told me that he had
given you the originals of the poems he had written here in the house . . . the ones about the
Karoo. The only copies we had were taken away
by the Special Branch and we never got them
back. I tried several times in London to get him to
remember them and write them down again but

he said no he couldn't do that, because they were yours. They were a gift to you and would be safe with you until the time came for them to be read. I think that time has come, don't you?

They've never been published. I've got a few early ones as well, but not enough for a book. That's what I want to do, collect them all together and publish them under the title he was going to give his book: *Rejoicings.*

(Pause, Marta says nothing.)

I just need to make copies. You can keep the originals and if there are any royalties they will go to Rebecca.

(Marta still says nothing.)

Is something wrong?

MARTA *(A long pause before she speaks)*: They're gone, Allison.

ALLISON: Gone? What do you mean?

MARTA: They got burnt.

ALLISON: Oh my God! What happened? Was there a fire?

(Marta again says nothing.)

Marta! What's the matter? Why don't you speak?

MARTA *(Struggling)*: It is really my fault, Allison. You see I didn't know all what she was feeling . . . I was just so upset . . . and then I hit her . . .

ALLISON: I don't know what you are talking about.

MARTA: The day we had the big fight in here, Rebecca and me.

REBECCA *(Quietly)*: I burnt them.

MARTA: It's all right, Rebecca, you don't have to . . .

REBECCA: No. I want to tell it.

Like Mommy said we was in here after the funeral of the old man, and there she was once again, polishing the table with her tears. I could see how she had tried to hold them back during the funeral when all the white people were looking at us with cruel eyes. I didn't know what to do. My mother was crying again and I didn't know what to do to stop it, what to say, how to help her. All I knew was that he was to blame. The man I couldn't call father was to blame, and I wanted to hit him like my mother had hit me. So when I ran out of here I went home. She kept all his letters and the papers he had given her in a box under her bed. I took them and a box of matches and I went out into the veld and burnt them. All of them. One by one. I watched them all turn into ash and smoke, out there in the veld.

MARTA: She didn't come home that night. I was worried out of my mind. Next morning I went to the police station. They found her on the road walking to Graaff-Reinet and brought her back to me. When I asked her why she was running away she told me what she had done. *(A helpless gesture)* All I could do was tell her that if she wanted so badly to get rid of him, she would have to burn her mother's heart as well.

ALLISON *(Bitterly)*: "The Fires of South Africa"! Amazing! That was going to be the title of a poem he tried to write in London. We had just watched a BBC program about the township riots. Houses and buildings burning, barricades in the street, uniforms and guns and those hideous armored cars everywhere, a pall of tear gas and smoke over everything. It ended, as it always does, with the image of a woman weeping.

(She tries to remember the poem) I think it went:

Fires of sorrow,
Fires of hate . . .

(Pause) And then something like:

Incendiary tears
Ignite our fate . . .

I'll look for it when I get back and go through his papers. There might be a few other things that I can pull together to make a small volume, but I certainly won't be calling it *Rejoicings.*

I must go and pack. When you are finished in here, Marta, come past the guest house and I will give you that copy of David's will.

(Allison starts to leave. At the entrance to the passageway she stops, turns back and speaks to Rebecca.)

For your soul's sake, Rebecca, I hope you know that what you did was terribly wrong. What you turned to ash and smoke out there in the veld was evidence of a man's love, for his country, for his people—for you! Don't reject it. That love was clean and clear and good! It was the best of him. For your soul's sake claim it, Rebecca. Rejoice in it! Because if you think you and your "new South Africa" don't need it, you are making a terrible mistake. You are going to need all the love you can get, no matter where it comes from.

(Allison leaves. After a few seconds of silence Marta begins carefully to put chairs back in their places and to tidy up a few other things in the room. She stops suddenly and looks around.)

MARTA: It's somehow different in here now, isn't it? Like . . . *(Trying to find words for what she feels)* Like why am I doing this? Why am I putting everything back so carefully in the place where it belongs? Because—ja, that's it!—because nothing in here has got a place where it belongs anymore. I didn't know a room could also die, but this one has.

You see he was the reason for everything in here, Bekkie. He gave it its life. Everything had its place because he was coming back. And that included me. From the day I was born I had my place in this room. Stinkwood Marta belonged in here as much as that table and chairs and everything else. So she swept and dusted and polished and waited. But that's all over now. This room is waiting for a new life, Bekkie, and you've got to give it that. You've got to be the reason now for everything in here.

(Marta sees that Rebecca has put her hands tentatively on the stinkwood table.)

Ja, beautiful hey! Can you feel how alive it is? You'll learn to love it as well, and don't worry, it will be different for you. It won't need your tears to make it shine.

(Pause. Breaking her mood) But that's enough for one day. Come, we must go.

(Wordlessly Marta and Rebecca start to leave. Rebecca has already disappeared down the passageway when Marta turns back for her bible and hymn book which she left on a side table. She pauses and looks around the room. The moment segues into a memory of the young Dawid on the night he first made love to her.)

DAWID *(Passionate and intensely alive, a sheet of paper in his hand)*: Listen to this!

(He plays with the names, exploring and enjoying them for their rich musicality:)

    Appolis, Arries, April
    Baartman, Baadjies, Bokbaard and Bruintjies
    Carelse
    Duimpies
    Goliath and Grootboom
    January, Japhta, Julies and Jantjies
    Kleinbooi
    Malgas, Muggels and Meintjies
    November
    Plaatjies, Persensie
    Sambok, September, Stuurman
    Vaaltyn, Voetpad, Vetbooi
    Witbooi . . .

Yes of course, names, and straight from a Karoo telephone directory. What's so wonderful about them? Come on, Marta! Take a couple and roll them around in your mouth and taste them . . . *(He demonstrates)* Jantjies . . . Jantjies . . . Jantjies and Bruintjies . . . Jantjies, Bruintjies and Duimpies . . . *(He smacks his lips)* They taste of the Karoo . . . sweet water and dry dust!

Close your eyes and play with "Arries" long enough and you'll hear that little whisper of relief when a little breeze stirs the leaves of the old bluegum tree at the end of a hot day. Do the same with "Vaaltyn" and you'll see the Karoo veld in the middle of a drought, gray and brittle, and if it's sweetness you want then play with "Marta" and "Barends" . . .

Marta Barends! When I roll that around in my mouth I taste Karoo food, Karoo sweetness. Warm crusty brown bread just out of the oven and honey, wild aloe honey, thorntree honey. Warm Bruin Brood en Doringboom Heuning!

Incredible isn't it . . . a poem . . . an almost perfect little poem and it comes straight out of a Karoo telephone directory! One more poem for the collection! I want it to be the first one. And it comes complete with a title: "A Karoo Directory."

Hell, Martha! This land of ours. So beautiful! But also so cruel! Sometimes I think old Eugene Marais was right in his "Song of South Africa": She gives nothing, but demands everything. Tears, the names of the dead, the widow's lament, the pleading gestures and cries of children . . . all mean nothing to her. She claims as her holy right, the fruits of endless pain.

No! Don't cry. It's only a poem, Marta . . . Marta Barends! . . . Warm brown bread and thorntree honey . . . Yes! You are all of that.

(The moment segues back into the present. Marta is standing at the table lost in her memory. Rebecca appears in the doorway. She stands silently for a second.)

REBECCA: Are you coming, Mommy?

MARTA: Yes . . . yes . . .
REBECCA: Are you all right?
MARTA: I'm fine. Come, let's go.

(The two women disappear down the passageway. We hear the front door open and close.)

END OF PLAY

Glossary

AFRIKAANS—One of the official languages of South Africa, developed from the seventeenth century Dutch

AFRIKANER—Descendants of the original Dutch settlers who arrived in 1652

AG, REBECCA—Oh, Rebecca

BOEREWORS—Farmer's sausage

DAWID—David (the "w" is pronounced as a "v" and the "a" is pronounced as the "a" in "father")

DEURMEKAAR—Confused

FREE STATE VLAKTES—Free State plains

HAAI SIESTOG!—Exclamation of sympathy

JOBURG—Johannesburg

KAROO—Semi-desert region in the center of South Africa

KOPPIES—Hills

MATRIC—Matriculation examination, at the end of the last year of high school

MEISIES—Young women

MOS—Afrikaans speech mannerism which adds emphasis to a statement

SKAAMTE—Shame

VELD—Plains

VRIEND OF VYAND—Friend or enemy

ATHOL FUGARD has been working in the theatre as a play-wright, director and actor since the 1950s. His plays have been produced throughout his native South Africa, as well as in major theatres across the United States and abroad. His previous works include *Blood Knot, Boesman and Lena, The Captain's Tiger, Cousins: A Memoir, Hello and Goodbye, A Lesson from Aloes, Marigolds in August, The Guest, "Master Harold"... and the boys, My Children! My Africa!, Notebooks: 1960–1977, Playland, A Place with the Pigs, The Road to Mecca, Statements* and *Valley Song.*